Eye to Eye with My Octopi

poems by

Richard Stevenson

Copyright© 2022 Richard Stevenson
ISBN: 978-93-95224-08-6

First Edition: 2022
Rs. 200/-

Cyberwit.net
HIG 45 Kaushambi Kunj, Kalindipuram
Allahabad - 211011 (U.P.) India
http://www.cyberwit.net
Tel: +(91) 9415091004
E-mail: info@cyberwit.net

No part of this book may be reproduced or transmitted in any form or by any means, electronic, mechanical, photocopying, or otherwise, without the express written consent of Richard Stevenson.

Printed at Repro India Limited.

What the critics say:

About WHY WERE ALL THE WEREWOLVES MEN?:

This book is utter nonsense. Delightful nonsense. ... Read one or two of these poems to a rowdy group of nine-year-olds, and you'll have their rapt attention. Read them to yourself and you'll chuckle at the imagery and adroit use of language. Stevenson has an ear for what children like without stooping to patronize. This is one for the young monsters of your household."

– David Bly, The Calgary Herald

About NOTHING DEFINITE YETI:

Stevenson evokes the nightmare world of dreams, in wit and humour, to create an engaging new folklore for the millennium. The young of all ages will find this book simply a whole lot of fun.

– Richard Olafson, Ekstasis Editions

About TAKE ME TO YOUR LEADER!:

The poems ... are more than entertainment: Maybe we really are the victims of a cosmic joke, pulled through a Loonie Tune wormhole patch. Maybe some of us have had a soul transfer. Whatever's happened one thing's certain: These poems are full of clever rhymes that will make you laugh out loud and even guffaw. It's a hip and inventive collection and Stevenson has an obvious affection for aliens. Joseph Anderson, his illustrator, seems to be in tune with the critters too. Besides the cover art, the book contains 20 wacky illustrations. Buy it for the kids; keep it for yourself.

– Lori Lavallee, Lethbridge Insider

Acknowledgements

Poems in this collection have previously appeared in the following e-zines and journals:

Bewildering Stories, Black Petals, Devour, Farther Stars From Here, Granfalloon, I Become The Beast, Poetry Pasta, Rune Bear, Scarlet Dragonfly Journal, SciFaikuest, The Siren's Call, The Starlight ScFaiku Review, Star*Line and Polar Starlight.

My thanks to the editors for their support of this endeavour.

Contents

Paranormal Paradiddle 7
Spoonbills in Minnesota 9
The Quagga 10
The Gumberoo 11
Roch Ness Monster 12
Beaman 13
The Iceman 14
Hairy Hominid 15
The Nimergar 16
Zantegeba 17
Lake Tianchi Monster 21
Crocottas's Gotta … 23
Upah 24
Giant Anaconda 26
Stikini 28
Djinn and Tonic 29
Homo floresiensis 32
The Ninki Nanka 35
The Ghostly Scarecrow of Chiang Rui 37
Cattle Mutilations 40
Beneath the Dulce Desert Sands 41
The Vampire of Highgate Cemetery 43
Terrible Touch 45
Slenderman 47
Shadowman 49
What if Caddy … 51
Sasquatch and Sex 53
Treeskinner 55
Giglioli's Whale 56
Fangalabolo 60
The Ug Wug 61
Pressie 63

Isugugumadevu	64
Tennessee Wild Man	66
MIB Couple at the Bar	67
Dingbat	70
Mhuwe	71
Corfu Island Creature	72
Huggin' Molly	73
The Black Stick Man	75
Bozho, the Madison Monster	76
Black Bird of Chernobyl	77
Dundas Island Blackflies	79
Tra Tra Tra Tra	80
De Loy's Ape	84
Darrel Dogigator	86
Red Rain	87
Qualupalik	89
The Kalanoros of Madagascar	90
Amali	92
Gwyllgi	93
Jorogumo	94
Homo Sapiens III	95
Paranormal Parasites	97
Big Gulp?!	100
Tunnepfiefer	101
Megalania Mania	103
The Slaugh	105
Gbahali (Bar Lye)	106
Kajanok	107
Hibagon	113
Reptoid Encounter	115
An Argentine Alien	117
Veggie Man	119
The Monster of Lake Totu	120
Yamakachi	121
Derrider Roadkill	122
Multiverses, eh?	123

Paranormal Paradiddle

Paranormal paradiddle
(Drum roll for aesthete geeks!)
Ain't gonna get cold feet, are we?
Come on. Grab some flashlights.
Bob and weave!
Ain't tryin' to deceive... .

Got photos, hairs, and footprints.
Got rotting globster DNA.
Got dermal ridges and smidges
of whoknowswhatkindastickymucusergoo.
All kinds of theories about whosits
and whatsits and woozles ... .
Ain't tryin' to confuse... .

What we lack in facts
we've made up in spades
of credible anecdotal reports.
Heck, we've got official forms!
Witnesses spyin' shape defyin' forms
and hairless melanin-deprived
melon head gorms.
Sorry for all the forms... .

Just tell us what you want.
Tell us what you truly need.
Tell us what to feed the citizenry.
We'll tell you on a need-to-know basis
everything we've gleaned so far
or wish you didn't know we knew –
redacted, of course. In triplicate at least.
Enough to bring you to your knees.

Spoonbills in Minnesota

Roseate Spoonbills
sighted in Minnesota?!
Florida has reached
its quota? Not enough
shrimp to go around?

Brrr, it's cold up here!
I can hear them gabbling
Let's get a spoonful
of medicine and flee this coop.
This place isn't fit for a goose!

The Quagga

Pity the Quagga –
lost more than its stripes
when it moved south.
The Dutch of South Africa
hunted them to extinction.

Zebra sans passport
unspooled its lot in life
as a non-Zebra
for years before earning
sub-zebra status. Not fair!

A horse is a horse
of course, as everyone knows.
The Quagga's stripes might
as well have been hoops,
hoops around a horse shoe pit.

The Gumberoo

Listen up, Buckaroo.
What I'm about to tell you
may save your life!

Many a greenhorn
has pooh poohed the story and
lived to regret it.

And I'm talking
about the lucky ones!
The ones that survived!

Gumberoos are bears
with tough furless hides.
Bullets bounce off them!

The only way to kill
the fearsome beast is to
burn it alive!

How you gonna do
that without starting
a forest fire?!

Worse luck, if you breathe
in the smoke, it'll coat
your lungs with rubber!

Yeah, Gumberoos –
if they don't get you first,
a ricochet might.

Roch Ness Monster

Corpse of a creature
found at Hollingsworth Lake
a five-foot pike?

What big teeth you have!
grannies expostulate.
Forget swimming here!

I can get a fist
into its mouth. Want me
to turn it inside out?

Monstrous sock puppet
or unknown cryptid hoser?
Let's see what it eats.

Beaman

Beaman –
hybrid bigfoot/wolf
hangs out in the woods
near Kansas City.

Large, sharp canines
and incisors!
The better to scarf you with
in Kansas *or* Missouri

Believe me!
If you're gonna hunt here,
you best bring
a skookum blunderbuss.

A laser sabre
might give you
a fighting chance
to vaporise him first.

Otherwise, you're
staying for dinner –
not as a guest;
more likely as *hors d'oeuvres*.

The Iceman

The iceman
mighta been
a nice man
but for the
damn weather!

Grew fur
outta necessity –
Not enough.
Succumbed.
Poor bugger.

Hairy Hominid

Hairy hominid
with protruding bulbous eyes –
not the Betty Davis kind.

Whaddaya want me
to say? It clocked us
for a city block!

Was big as a bear.
Covered in black fur ...
Suddenly bipedal!

Not a 'squatch –
Furry, not hairy ...
with bulbous mantis eyes.

Finally dropped back!
Pulled four yards of cotton
on that job!

No skid marks
on my underwear ...
Musta puckered right up!

The Nimergar

The Nimergar –
nasty three-foot archers
on our arses.
Used poison arrows;
got up with the sparrows!

Scrawny necks –
If a guy could get
his hands around him,
he'd whip their Wyoming butts.
Yell, "Who's the putz now?!"

Coulda shared the work
raising crops with us, but no!
They'd rather shoot first ...
Try out this golf ball launcher!
Here, let me turn the others on.

Zantegeba

Zantegeba
(he with big paws)
Baboon-like creature
from Mali said to attack
and rape unwary women.

Festival fave now –
So fun for the men to chase
the ladies with stick
forearms, as the women shriek,
pretend to escape their claws.

Fake booger no doubt –
Easily fended off with grace,
Saves men precious face;
Save a woman from the beast,
get past first base at least.

The Cardiff Giant
was made of gypsum –
a total gyp – and then some

*

Does Big Rhodey
have enough tuliewumps?
Homeless 'squatches now?

*

Dire wolf's in dire straights –
eat more humans or end up
stuffed or in a zoo

*

Mane-less man-eater
lions lay low in the veldt –
have sumptuous pelts

*

blue tigers?!
blue as the horizon
sans fluffy sheep clouds

*

Lau like to loaf –
forty feet of languorous coils
can afford to go limp

*

Sasquatch T-shirt:
"Social Distancing
World Champion"

(found senryu)

*

A petroglyph
would have it so:
Sproat Lake Monster lives!

Ain't doin' stunts though:
a pair of parallel humps
and anal asterisk *adieu*

(for John Kirk)

Lake Tianchi Monster

Elasmosaurus
don't need a chorus,
great hullabaloo
made over the length of his
flexible reptile neck.

He'd as soon you bob
for apples in a bucket
as make a ruckus
over his tumble turns
and fancy manoeuvres.

Still, it behooves him
to put in an appearance,
to maintain the flow
of tourist dollars and awe –
long as you feed him fresh fish.

Your wish: his command!
He'll stand on his flukes,
grin and look cute for
a pop tart or fish fillet.
What the heck, stroke his neck …

It's dope; it's o.k.
He'll grin and slap a flipper
round yer sodden shoulder,
snuggle close for a serpent
and homey selfie, bro!

No kidding!
Back flips for Tim Bits!
Maybe a quick toot
from the ol' pooper chute
in lieu of formal *adieu*...

Crocottas's Gotta ...

Crocotta's a dog
the size of a mule
with leopard spots.
She's gotta check all the boxes
for cryptid cash box receipts!

Why the lack of noise
about this hungry beast?
No mention of homo s kebabs
or head-hulled brain cheeze.
No one begging on their knees.

That because so few
escape to tell the tale?
So few stopped to measure
her shiny incisors
before ending up inside her?

Upah

Sumatra's Upah –
a foot-long green centipede –
has a wicked bite.

Venomous critter
screams like a cat in distress
when you pick it up.

Just don't! With gloves
or a stick. It'll twist free,
rear back and bite you.

You won't be going
anywhere after that
but flat on your back.

The toxin will soon
swell your tissues til you look
like the Michelin Man,

Arms angled from
your sides like you were
hoping to flap wings.

And — oh! — how it stings!
Burns! Makes you squirm
right out of your skin

til you're as pink
as a newborn, hoping
to grow a thick hide.

Giant Anaconda

(with a nod to Ogden Nash)

Don't get too fonda
the giant anaconda
He'll squeeze you to paste
before he succumbs to drugs
or points a nose in yer cage.

Can't bonk or zonk 'im,
winch 'im up on a spool
Huge snake Houdini
a hundred feet long
fat as a sewer pipe

gonna swallow ya
in a coupla' bites –
Don't apologize
for bolting his food;
belches and farts a lot too!

He might wrap you
in a coupla' coils –
fast food for dinner
for the missus and boys –
smiles plump as Christmas puddings …

or nurse a growing
bump of the lotta ya
in the setting sun ...
shit out your bones
in sequenced single pellets.

There ya go!
Ninety-eight cents worth,
allowing for inflation.
Grind it up for beach sand
or add it to yer tooth paste.

Stikini

Stikini –
owls with human faces –
enjoy changing places.

Barf up their guts
and hide 'em
for later retrieval.

Then they fly as owls
pluck human heads
from sleeping babes.

Stikini ain't teeny
Can't tempt 'em
with beans and weenies.

Nope. Gotta be hearts
little kid tickers
pure and juicy.

Yum yum!
When sophontsofied
they re-bolt their human guts –

Swallow 'em whole
like peas buried
in mashed potatoes.

Can't taste
the human guts that way
Can't take 'em most days … .

Djinn and Tonic

The Djinn don't come in bottles
though they may play hide and seek
with them. Treat them like bowling pins.

The Djinn disobeyed Allah's orders
to become subservient to man
cos they thought they were the superior species.

They thrived on plasma –
a fourth form of matter
like an intelligent shape-shifting gas.

Could pass as people, dogs,
whatever host form they chose.
Pretend to be man's best friend.

Don't trust 'em. Any time
they give a gift to man
or pretend to spare or save him,

the fee down the road comes due,
and it ain't a few pasta dishes
or piastas, brother, but your hide!

Djinns get right inside you,
steal the controls from your very will.
Get you to sin or even kill for them.

Djinns don't need no tonic
to make 'em palatable either –
and can flow like blood in yer veins.

Djinns ain't no genies, bro,
though the three wishes meme likely came
from a distortion of some make-a-deal event.

Don't even attempt negotiation!
Again, they'll promise you the moon,
make you faint and swoon with promises.

Don't invite a Djinn in for gin and tonics.
Don't even spell the word in Phonics.
Don't even think or read of them.

Consciousness of Iblis and his evil clan
is enough to invite them into yer pia mater
where they'll start to shape yer thoughts.

The trouble is how to spot 'em. To learn
to trust your instincts if you're not sure... .
Best not cosey up to strangers anyway.

I know it doesn't sound too charitable.
One should reach out to help one's fellow man,
but only if he's on the level, truly needy

and not some snake in the reeds
like Satan. Remember Iblis' other name
is Shaitan. Yer one syllable away from sin.

Maybe drop the name. See if yer guy
flinches or seems to get uncomfortable.
If he does, bolt your door; loose the hounds.

You gotta know Iblis' boys are making the rounds.
Better give 'im a touch of the Timpsons
(a boot in the ass, a shove, by any name.)

Homo floresiensis

The discovery in 2004
of a new species of Homo
on the Indonesian island of Flores
got a lot of folks talking.

The three-foot hominids
who lived alongside homo s
as recently as 13,000 years ago
was a hairy hunter/gatherer.

At first, we thought the skeletons
found in a cave were those
of small children, but, no,
they were skeletons of fully-grown adults!

Adults with spears or other tools
or vegetarians who gathered
nuts in May? Who knows?
But the prospect of other hominids

like Cro- Magnon or Neanderthal,
maybe even Gigantopithecus,
who stood better than ten feet tall
may give more credence to Yeti *et al.*

Maybe Ebu Gogo and Orang Pendek
are close relatives and not just
gangly knuckle-draggin' orangutans
or other lower order primates.

Maybe Homo floresiensis
brought home the bacon
with fruit and salad greens.
Contemplated his navel on cave walls.

Maybe a three-foot guy on a walkabout
had a lot more to think about
than what four-footed mammals
he ought to bring home for supper.

Maybe bein' just a little guy
forced him into a better diet
than carnivore meat and tubers,
got him into home decorating.

Once he didn't have to walk so far
or outsmart root vegetables
or keep an eye out for predators,
he could spend more time at home.

Better Homes and Gardens
made for better spousal relations.
Got him tinkerin' with other tools
than spears and bow and arrows.

Maybe Sasquatch learned to cook
and made kick-ass salads,
when he wasn't out pawing fish
out of lakes, prying bivalves off of rocks.

Could sasquatch be Gigantopithecus?
Could Bigfoot just need a podiatrist
or cobbler to make the next pay grade
and catch up with us? He ain't as ornery

or disagreeable maybe. If we'd just stop making plaster casts and gathering cack and get on with the business of sharing resources and window ledge pies, maybe... .

The Ninki Nanka

The Ninki Nanka of Gambia
ain't lookin' for the limelight, babe.
Too many cryptozoologists' boots
have come slogging through their swamp
in search of selfie and serpent shots.

They tromp down the reeds,
leave peacock feather eyes
of spilled gasoline on the water,
leave glass bottles bobbing
before they fill up and sink.

Whaddaya want the Ninki to do with them?
Collect 'em for re-cycling? Like they'd
ever show up with a shopping cart
full of bottles for redeemable tokens
they can't even use. As if, Sherlock!

Some idiot bonked one Ninki kid on the noggin
with an empty beer can the other day,
and their finny prey keep washin' ashore
with six-pack plastic holders
wrapped around gills and fins!

Can't these semi-sentient hominids
pick up their debris? They're smart
enough not to shit their pants
when someone pulls on one of their teats.
Now they want *them* doing tumble turns?!

Why don't the Ninki just swim over and barf
in their boats if these humans are so keen on ambergris?
They've got nothing better to do than offer up
their toe nail clippings and relatives' skulls
from their watery graves? BE-have!

The Ninka Nanka aren't usually mean,
but are getting pretty annoyed.
Might just sink a few pleasure cruisers
and whomp up some homo s kebabs
over an open fire – if they had digits.

Never mind. They could just drown us
and serve up our gibblets cold.
Human brains make a nice paté
and aren't so hard to hull from the skull.
Why not heart and brains on the half shell?

We're already half-baked anyway.
Yeah, nards and nibbley bits on crackers –
Maybe some human intestine hummus –
Nice trade-off for trout or weeds and eel,
if yer a hungry little Ninka Nanka, maybe … .

The Ghostly Scarecrow of Chiang Rui

Huay Nam Rak –
an armless red-eyed cryptid
hovered above the rice.

Trained its fiery orbs
on me as if to implore
my help with something.

I fled. Knew someone
above my pay scale
should see what I saw!

Show and Tell critter
for some UFOlogist
to stow inside a bottle.

Maybe not just then,
but before they could settle
on what to feed it.

Turned its nose up
at dry rabbit food, lettuce.
Wouldn't let us near.

Like it hadda be
Tim Bits or pizza –
what the hell?! It died.

Now resides
in a stout clear bottle
of formaldehyde.

***

slinky Silguey –
Commanda Salamanda
of many BC lakes –
slippery when wet
slipperier to net

*

whaddaya mean
there's no Shoe Swap here?!
Centipede's feet hurt!
He's come miles. Needs to park
all hundred sore dogs at least!

    (Shuswap, BC)

*

Nuk Luk would rather
chase frozen horse pucks
than dig for geoducks.*　　　　　* pronounced *gooey ducks*
Every time he closes on one,
it squirts saltchuck in his eyes

Megaconda
likes to hug with all his coils
is fonda goils too

*

eye to eye
with my octopi
I'd have to say
our guys aren't so shy
as twice wise

*

enough with
the blunderbuss, Gus!
you don't want us
to monkefy yer mast,
not with eight arms to grasp!

Cattle Mutilations

At first, the military brass didn't balk
at the abduction of a few head of cattle.
Even helped ETs load 'em in black helicopters.

But then the saucers made the job
more efficient, ETs started abducting cattle
from every state in the union, and humans too!

All the while, we tried to reverse engineer
the technology that made saucers fly –
so neat, so fleet. Biopsied dead saucer folk.

And how do we reveal the plan to humankind
now that the reptoids and their minion greys
have had their stories implode? Confess?

Too late for that! Maybe it's no big hairy deal
the reptoids will thrive for a time before
the temperatures exceed their lizard needs.

Enter the cockroach. Maybe it doesn't mind
rapid mutation. Can stomach a few
radioactive pellets and polluted water.

However things turn out, it's clear fear
never bought us a spot on Parnassus.
Even the dinosaurs will have had a better run.

Beneath the Dulce Desert Sands

Deep beneath the Dulce desert sands –
maybe miles deep, and off-limits
to most military personnel, a secret lab exists.

May well have existed for eons,
the site of wild genetic experiments
in which the greys, soulless flesh robots –

much later in collusion with top human scientists –
tried to extract abductees' souls, and soaked
in blood baths of animal and human body parts!

Seems the Greys have no digestive tracts.
No anus from which to excrete waste,
digest food or drink. They must absorb energy

through the skin, wallow amid blood and guts –
likely at the beck and call of reptoids
who've had a hand in our species' evolution.

A whistleblower, whose name shall remain
anonymous, came to learn the reptoids
had altered the DNA of Neanderthals,

Cro-Magnon Man ... literally created Homo Sapiens,
and all the world's major religions,
the concepts of heaven and hell, the whole shebang.

All to keep us on the track of an afterlife
while they abducted thousands they imprisoned
in the dreaded cages of the deepest level seven.

Now Dulce just looks like an ordinary small town –
3,000 inhabitants, clean streets, ample services… .
No one suspected a thing, until the brass learned

they had been deceived. Bought the deal
of an exchange of technologies for cow parts –
saucers, saucer propulsion, lasers, post-it notes…

Few ever got to level 7. One who snuck down
blew the whistle and, in 2017, the military
planted an atomic bomb 4,000 feet below the ground.

It blew up plenty. Not them. We lost that war.
And now greys and reptoids own an expanding underground
warehouse of captured souls and animals.

Worse than Mistress Bathory who bathed in the blood
of blessed virgins in an attempt to regain
her youth and beauty, and killed hundreds.

These greys are taking thousands – perhaps
hundreds of thousands over the millennia!
Their plans: to steal our souls and our planet.

To create a series of over-souls to envelope
their spindly, big cabeza-headed bodies.
To terraform our planet to their specifications.

Could direct a wholescale invasion any day –
all run from under the Archuleta Mesa,
below lil old Dulce, New Mexico – and we know!

The Vampire of Highgate Cemetery

Seen outside the gates
or just inside, a tall, thin man
in top hat and long frock

says "Good evening, sir."
You're disoriented, can't find
your way to your dead friend's plot.

Just nod, but can't fail to notice
the closer this pale homunculus gets,
the more exhausted you become.

He's not going to suddenly sink
his incisors in your neck but
his eyes flame red when he looks at you.

Sunken cheeks, wan complexion.
No widow's peak or aversion
to crosses apparently. Wrinkled lips.

Could have stepped out of the pages
of a nineteenth-century vampire epic –
even floated through the mist on cue.

But this is psychedelic sixties' London.
Guy could just be some junkie
with a soft spot for cement cribs.

You manage to stumble to a bus,
get home, have a shower, take a nap.
Still feel depleted. The man's face

shows up in your dreams repeatedly.
Always getting closer, closer;
his skin rosier, plumper...

ParAbnormal parasite? Doesn't bite
or suck blood from your jugular maybe,
but he drains you nonetheless.

Be careful what you wish for
if you come at midnight a decade on.
Garlic will just make you stink.

Gonna whistle for a Bobbie to come
whack the ghost's coconut? Good luck.
You might want to bring a change of underwear.

Probably more useful than a silver bullet
or stout sharp stake anyway.
Bring a sleeping bag, tooth brush, tooth paste.

If you're going to traipse into the constabulary
the next day, better to approach the desk
with fresh breath and a you-won't-believe-this pitch,

It's not like no one's heard your story
or ever met the ghost before, just so you know.
Take your time. Don't stutter over clutter.

Tell your story simply and plainly.
Get ready for a rich refrain:
souvenir shop's just around the corner.

Terrible Touch

In a tent in the woods
of Mt. Washington I fell asleep.

Not a peep or soft batting
of a Polyphemus moth

against a tent flap, yet
I felt I was being observed.

Fitful sleep. Tired the next day –
Chalked in down to nervous stress.

Next night, not so lucky –
Hat men! Shadow persons with

index fingers on my navel
like they were gassing up!

So tired. Could barely make out features ...
Fedoras, no eyes or noses ... Yelled "NO!"

They vanished! Into thin air as they say ...
Better print my story or you'll be sorry ...

I was wide awake when I saw
what I saw! Not much, but the touch...

You had to feel that! A subtle zap,
the feeling of being sucked up a straw!

That was no dream or hallucination!
Look! Rings like Saturn's around my eyes!

Don't sleep much now. Cat nap
with feelers flexin'. A few hours …

Just don't enter the room suddenly.
I'll be dukes up, standing in my BVDs!

Slenderman

Slenderman –
ain't no insurance
bump and fender man,
no smooth howdy doody
buck-toothed rube.

Ain't no 3-D
nuisance or accessory,
just a 2-D flat
easy-to-put-away
toffee-flexive guy.

What trouble can I
possibly get you in?
I'm just a toffee
s-t-r-e-t-c-h-a-b-l-e gif,
a sociable social meme.

Got no features!
Got no face!
If I had 'em
I'd just lose 'em or
stretch 'em out of shape.

Got no gender to bend,
no reason to offend,
no ill-gotten gains,
no smelly remains,
just a toffee body

Nothin' fat or cloddy.
Slenderman! That's me!
I'll tender all affection
to my soft center…
Don't mention it.

Shadowman

Who needs vampiric
hoes and haberdashery?
Who needs bat and wolf familiars
when you can taffy-take a
whole meme on the Internet
with pseudopodic grace
without features or a face?

I was born on the Web!
You think I don't have tentacles?!
Shadowman you call me,
2-D toffee-stretchin' gif
on the Internet. Safe as milk
as Captain Beefheart would put it.
More fun than Mr. Roger's Neighbourhood!

It's a perfect day on the Internet...
Watch me come with my intergalactic
magnet of mirth and merriment.
Invaginate into your tender children,
Bud 'em off their reality and into mine.
No muss, no fuss; no bite, no blood.
Yer incubus/succubus toffee tosser.

Gotta love these kiddy rubes!
Pop their heads and quaff their blood
if I could. They're so sippy sweet!
Don't have to though. Gotta better move…
Yep, Just extend another pseudopod,
swallow you whole, bod by bod.
I get bigger, with no Identikit.

What if Caddy ...

What if Caddy had a hankerin'
to head up north for herring,
trolled Departure Bay one day?

I have a hunch he'd stay for lunch –
maybe until school let out for the day
and all the herring kids came out to play.

But would he scrunch up a buncha humps,
show us his finesse at tumble turns for Tim Bits
or show us the asterisk of his arse?

Maybe he'll bestow a fish fart or two,
Barf up a greasy tentacle in ambergris
from last night's poorly digested meal ...

What? You're gonna gather it up?
Put it in a bag and freeze it
until you can sell it by the cube?!

Eugh! So sin-crude of you!
What's Cadborosaurus tentacle puke
worth on the open market anyway?

Not that I'd countenance the thought
of adding turpines and herbs to get
a good perfume. Let alone gather it up!

*Your secret's safe, but eugh!
The very thought of herring and octopi broth...
condensed serpent sauce... Who knew...?*

Sasquatch and Sex

So what's with all the lover's lane
drop-in scenes? Steamy windows,
teens making the beast with two backs,
when – BOOM! – a 'squatch lands on the hood!

Voyeurs that draw sexual energy
from us? Make the radio station
turn to static? Suck the juice
outta batteries, disable all media?

Really?! Goatman, Bolam Beast too...
Maybe they're not even corporeal entities –
sometimes they're only *seen* in 2-D!
Gorge on our orgone energy to exist.

Or maybe the Greek satyr is no myth!
Goatman and the satyr are the same
paranormal parasite. Hoppin' in and out
of wormholes. Sucking the life out of us!

They don't suck our blood or tear us
limb from limb to get at our giblets
or hull skulls to get at our paté brains.
They just drain our orgone batteries!

Maybe they're shape-shifters to boot!
We're talking parallel universes ...
Permeable membranes in time ...
Refugees from some other planet maybe?

Maybe ETs are rescuing *them*
from one doomed planet
and droppin' 'em off in the tulies here ...
Wood, caves, water, prey –

What the hey! I've heard stranger tales
on radio, TV, vidz, DVDs, the Web ...
It's not a new idea. One the cops
oughta cop, I thought, and booked it!

They bought our story. Others' since.
Whatever boogie man you wanna insert,
add hair and bulk and a byline's worth.
Somethin's sucking us dry. T'ain't 'squatches...

Treeskinner

First spotted near Matranovák, Hungary –
sometimes referred to as the European
Yeti or Bigfoot, but thinner, lankier,
with knee-reaching arms, monkey face.

A surviving Pliopithecus or relative
with whitish-grey fur? Nocturnal
mischief maker. Avoids flashlights,
human thrill seekers. Fleeter deker.

Hangs in abandoned mines, near
limestone cracks and crannies.
Grabs, throws, eats with dextrous mitts
because they're handy … .

You could try leaving a hand of bananas
or bag of apples to show you're a fellow
friendly hominid. Maybe start a little
campfire; roast weenies and marshmallows.

I betcha he doesn't get a chance
to eat many of those. Who knows?
Could be a holiday hit maybe, A treat.
Something to make him pull up a stump

and set a spell with you –
Long as you put the bangsticks away.
Don't let him see any flashing metal.
No gun, no flashlight. Use few words.

Giglioli's Whale

Distinguishing feature: two dorsal fins.
(No known whale has two dorsal fins.)
Mutant humpbacks with mangled dorsal
have been known to grow an extra one, true,
and the rhinoceros dolphin has two.

Seldom seen since Enrico Hillyer Giglioni,
zoologist aboard the **Magenta**, spotted her
on September 4th, 1897. Sixty feet long –
too big for a dolphin; definitely a
baleen-feeding behemoth of some sort.

Nice to think a whale species could have
evaded us this long. Never harpooned,
never caught up in a net; never taken
humans for a tow before breaking free;
never spouted sea spume in our faces.

A creature of good graces maybe.
Let us have a good long gander at her
before duck-diving for a trench,
using her powerful front flippers
to pull herself out of mischief's way.

Having never been harpooned or caught,
she had no reason to attempt escape, maybe;
just tagged alongside mid-ship and grinned.
Maybe even waved a how-do-you-do before
rubbing barnacled bellies, snorting her adieu.

So Mr. Gigllioni gets the tag, should the whale
suddenly appear again. In *case* she does—
to save face in the race to have his own name
added to Linnaeus' line-up of once-cryptid,
now-accepted species. His own stay against death.

Put your dukes up!
I'd bet on the octopus
with eight fast gloves
lotsa lubricated glide
in his slippery slide

*

toss our octopus
a set of bagpipes –
he'll learn to play 'em
or lovingly persuade her
to doff her tartan jammies

*

the Allegewi
like their victims chewy
overweight humans
need not worry or despair
just bring extra underwear

*

twenty-foot long,
one-ton croc, Gustave's belly
was full of watches
and jewelry when he died –
a real gourmand our Gustave.

*

African Bullfrogs
gott a wicked bite!
Hang on like burdocks
the size of bowling balls.
Won't let go without a bonk.

*

Booger Bear's bigger
than the biggest Grizzly Bear
and just as ornery.
Short-faced bear, eh?
The better to bite yer butt.

*

Auli's no mermaid
sprawling on a Denmark rock.
Nah. She's a rolly poley dugong
who digs fresh water, dude
Ain't got no attitude

*

Fangalabolo

Fangalabolo's
Malagasy for
"that which seizes the hair."

A whole toupée?!
That's gotta be a Malagasy
Fangalabolo Festival!

For thieving big bats
on the natty nimble take,
a whole nest topper! Top that!

The Ug Wug

The Ug Wug's gotta mug
only a mother could love:
seal-salmon hybrid thing –

More like a pug who swam
too close to the dam and
rammed his snout into a wall.

Thirty feet long, without
accordioned snout. Likes to hang
about the famous Reversing Falls

where the severe tides cause
the river to change directions
twice a day. Corral confused trout

in the topsy turvy turnover
of waves. Flashes a finny grill
grin of six-inch pointy teeth.

Said to make his home in some
grotty cave beneath the waves.
Blamed for a lot of missing kayakers

and cannoodlers in the region –
since I don't know when. A while.
Best not drop by to check on

his relatives' longevity. Could be
the death of you. And Ug Wugs, as a rule,
are not wont to bolt their food.

They chew and chaw away
at all the dingly dangly bits of you
before hulling your skull for your brain.

It especially likes homo s brains –
loves the lovely grey folds and rivulets,
the two peach halves that cleave

so well! Scrumpdillyicious!
on the shell or mashed into a paste
betweeen slow-moving incisors!

Gotta have some! Right now! Inside her!
Little fish brains will hardly suffice
with ego-seasoned homo s brains about!

Pressie

Pressie ain't the least impressed
with yahoos in speed boats
who pursue her for candid
serpent/ hoser cell phone shots.

She's not as famous as Chessie
or Nessie or Ogopogo maybe,
but nor does she wish to be.
Let her swim or bob or snog

in an underwater grotto with
her main squeeze, Peter.
Peter and Pressie prefer to be
left alone in their moiling coils.

Press your point though and they
will bite your boat in two,
drown you and cart your sad
carcass off to the cave for dinner.

Never let it be said
they're inhospitable!
Human dinner guests are welcome
after a steady ho hum diet of fish.

Isugugumadevu

Isugugumadevu –
takes about as long to say
as the creature takes to chew.

Has a snake's head atop
a long neck like Mokele Mbembe's
and skookum big lizard legs.

(Note to self: Don't scale trees
in an effort to escape this one.
Don't just gawk and gape.)

Maybe s-l-o-w-l-y back up
rather than beat a hasty retreat,
draw attention bending leaves.

Let him scarf a caiman or
unfortunate antelope that loped
into the wrong river scene before you.

Forget the beast's dentition.
You'll be wishin' he didn't
catch the glint off yer pearly whites

and swing its big saurian head
around to snap you off yer pegs.
Isugugumadevu likes human meat.

Messy diner though. Only goes for
the brain and gizzards, leaves yer hide
pretty well intact. A sad, empty sack.

Tennessee Wild Man

Tennessee Wild man
had folks completely flummoxed.
More human than ape ...
Folks would jibber and gape
if you put 'im in a cage.

Couldn't kill and place
a stuffed one on display—
too outré, uncool,
probably criminal, eh? –
and likely covered in mites.

Photos are blurry –
he's always in a hurry
to escape the frame.
Sure is furry though;
piquant too, I have to say.

MIB Couple at the Bar

They came in close to closing –
Two maybe. I didn't pay
much attention to 'em at first.

Tall, anemic lookin'. Thin lips,
high cheekbones and domes:
guy in a fedora, woman in ill-fitting wig.

Dressed in all- black clothes
as it turned out, but weren't Goths:
more wrong era shabby chic geeks.

Natasha and Boris Baddanoff.
Each ordered a draft but
didn't drink. Just stared at me.

Didn't blink.
Didn't speak.
Didn't get up for a piss.

And when they did leave,
they left their untouched beer
glowing like lanterns on the table.

Next day I've got Strep,
feel half-past dead. Just know
I've got to get to a hospital!

Know this: we're livestock, baby!
Alien property. They suck on us
Like all-day suckers, believe it!

They made us and occasionally
need to thin the herd with
bacteria and viruses. No, Cyrus,

I'm not joking! We got Neanderthal
and Cro-Magnon splices in our
Homo s. genes. We're hybrids, honey!

Cruise around from mall to mall,
thinkin' we're all that and a
bag of chips. So hip, so cool.

But we're just cattle chewin' cud,
workin' up a big bolus of words,
movin' from stall to stall.

They've got us where they want us –
accessible, each family in its
little house and paddock.

Are busy grabbin' sperm and ova,
monkey mixin' alien and human DNA
to create Homo s. three. Yes sir!

Gaunt, grimacing grey/human aliens
got all the levers. High achiever types
with no fashion sense or need of us.

We're property. Spare parts specimens.
Might as well be a rack of tires
with our expiry date stamped on our foreheads.

All-season radials: gotta plane that water
doin' what we oughter do:
Consume! Consume! Consume!

Be fat enough come June.
Ready to de-bone or juice,
put up for winter in some saucer pantry or other,

I don't wonder. They got
their own shrink wrap
and packing protocols.

Lotta folks plum disappear!
May be flash-frozen and stored
for later retrieval for all we know.

All I know is they made me sick.
I was just some eye candy lolly
they sucked on with their eyes.

They left their drinks, but, sho-nuff,
sucked the energy outta me! Probably
took all my antibodies to boot!

I ain't half the guy I was
a year ago. Emaciated, weak... .
Still in recovery, and they'll be back!

Dingbat

Dingbat's done scarfed
yer ammo, Andy –
Ya left the damn door unlocked again!

He's scarfed cartons of cartridges
like boxes of metal Smarties,
ya damn fool! Scooped up

yer can of gasoline too.
Look! Soon be swoopin' down,
sprayin' us with bullets from his mouth,

no doubt! But check out the one
on display in The Friendly Buckhorn pub.
Wings out, as if just landing –

three-pointer buck it is too –
if that's the right word for a buck/
owl cross on a raptor run.

Only costs a buck to see. C'mon!
Owner got tired of watching patrons
blow smoke in his feathered face.

Put it in a nook. Back room closet
or somethin'. Dunno where but
it's only a buck, less than a pack of cigs.

You wanna see or what?
It's not just a stuffed owl
with a scowl and belly for Benjamins!

Mhuwe

A man-eating ice giant
of Lenape legend, according
to Ranker.com anyway –

Not a lot of reportage
given the beast's appetite
for humans. Most

guttural utterances are
swallowed whole while
Mhuwe pops yer head

like a bottle cap
clean off your neck and shoulders,
gulps his glut of yer gouting blood.

Bring food! Decent scoff,
Not just fast food pucks or pockets.
Feed 'em right, he might

turn back into a human. Really!
Chips he'll squeeze to dust
in the bag and toss to the ground.

No. No. No. Forget ground round
or any of its sub-species
of mystery meat. Deer, fish maybe …

Maybe an assortment of tender vittles
for puck-lipped, wrinkly-faced
omnivores you chance to meet.

Corfu Island Creature

Alas, not a surviving member
of the genus *Ambulcetus*,
Zeuglodon's ancient ancestor.

Not some flat-snouted dolphin
mutated by nuclear waste
or pasty-faced dugong or manatee.

Looks more like it would quack
than take a sizable bite out of you –
I dunno – jovial, rolly poley –

More Disney than dino, you know…
Sighted twice off the coast of Greece …
Really a plastic freeboard fender.

Sorry it was no mind-bending,
genus-bending dolphin/hippo hybrid.
Coulda fetched a cool razbutnik or two.

The photo doesn't do it justice.
You wanna reach out, pat it three times
on its gentle rubber bobbing head.

Huggin' Molly

Abberville, Alabama is her hang,
and she ain't no **Evening in Paris** Granny
Spritzer you wanna hug or kiss
or shuffle on the dance floor with.

No sir! She's damp, rank, and skanky –
a skinny bag of brittle bones
with a vice-like grip and breath
that could knock a bird off its perch!

Kids beware! Avoid any tallow-faced,
dark-clothed, wide brim-hatted
or dark hoodie-wearin' hag at your door.
She not only wants the floor —

She wants to SCREAM in your ear!
Pollute your lungs with her
pestilent, sewer-spawned breath.
It'll stun you speechless and she'll

have yer cowerin' piss-jammied
body in a sack, snap! Just like that!
Haul you off to some rank grotto or cave
where she'll pluck yer eyeballs for her drink ...

Nibble off your ears and noses,
yer dainty fingers and dangly bits
before you know you've got no fingers
or toes. Nothin' to wiggle or snag a cell phone

to call home to Mom or Dad on –
just a crunchy bon bon she might
mack on for an *aperitif* or after-
dinner snack, after she hulls yer skull... .

The Black Stick Man

The Black Stick Man
prefers back streets and alleys
to well-trafficked, well-lit places.

Slides by you without malice,
though some claim they feel
menace and malevolence thick as fog

when they pass on wintery roads.
The creatures have no discernable features,
look like Giacometti figures in a mist.

Think of the sound a dying battery makes
when the car just won't start.
The last few whirs and disgruntled grumbles.

You might not be able to get out of bed
the next day. Or will drag yourself
to the sink to gaze on your sunken orbs.

Big black Saturn size rings
around your slitted eyes. Big surprise
after your usual eight-hour sleep.

Give 'em a safe distance of ten feet
and wear Covid masks outdoors
if you spot one coming your way.

You might not get or spread a virus
but this guy's sack of woe is thicker
than molasses at forty below.

Bozho, the Madison Monster

Bozho of Lake Mendotas, Wisconsin
may be Champ and Ogopogo's cousin –
a saucy serpentine trickster rake
spotted in Monona and Waubesa Lakes,
maybe Kengonsa Lake, Mudlake too.
Good luck catchin' 'im fer yer zoo.

Folks here have had enough yahoo types
traipsing past their "No Trespassing" signs.
Have started erecting fences to protect
their favorite cryptid lake denizen.
Well, what the heck, saurian or snake,
'e's got as much right to fish a lake

as we sorry ass homo sapiens do.
So 'e's still a cryptid. Boo hoo.
Leave ol' Bozho alone. No cameras, cell phones.
Park those prong-tongued devils at home.
Let Bozho tip a few canoes, swat a few yahoos
out of their doubting canoodling noodles.

Bozho, short for Winnebozho –
Nanabozho, if you hail from farther north.
Civilized lake citizen: don't trample the grass.
Don't leave empties or recyclable trash.
So, sorry, no selfie and serpent autographs.
No science roll calls. No straining giraffes.

Black Bird of Chernobyl

Days before the Chernobyl Reactor Meltdown
several Ukrainian workers reported seeing
a mothman-like creature with blazing red eyes.

No neck, with tea saucer-sized eyes
appearing to stare out of its chest!
Hairy body, eight feet tall!

Ain't a Batsquatch though:
its twelve-foot wingspan was feathered
not black bald or furry. Long furry arms though...

Nothin' you'd wanna have snatch you
or drop you to crack your noggin
on sidewalk or street!

Lawn or fence don't look more inviting
from thirty feet either. Better beat it!
Get in the car and vamoose!

Cops took down the story,
Sent it out by e-mail to
all personnel and out their bowels.

A bolus of words got masticated
and swallowed by everyone
over beer and pizza off-shift.

Still, the pile of paper only grew.
No EYES ONLY copies flew the coop
to upper-crustin' operatives.

Might as well stamp the pile "Past Due"
or "Forget It." Beats workin' in
the Cold File basement dungeon for months!

No one's gonna hang at the Chernobyl
Cop Shop anyway. Birds gone: we're gone –
Lest we start growin' feathers too!

Did it snag you or make off with
your pet beagle? No? Yer good then –
No cracked noggin. No Lada snatch.

You hadda close encounter, yeah?
Gotta good one for the bar after dark.
Might fetch you a few free vodka tonics!

No crime has been committed.
Write a book. Get on Ropeadope
with the rest of the schmoes. Take a number… .

Dundas Island Blackflies

No wonder they haven't been classified:
just to set foot on the island is to invite
clouds of five- or six-inch hungry flies
to come and dine on your sorry hide.

They'll fly off with veritable chunks of you –
and siphon yer blood like teenagers
on a milkshake. I kid you not, Holmes!
Your eyes will swell shut; then where will you be?

Better have someone in a Hazmat suit
come cart you off to the hospital.
Heading there by yourself in a canoe?
Your funeral. Pretty hard to paddle without sight.

Red head. Red tail tip. Yellow band
around the middle of their abdomens:
you won't soon forget their appearance.
Think sharp tweezer-like mandibles.

Paddling in shorts, sandals, and T-shirt?
You'll look like glistening hamburger meat,
assuming there's enough of you left
to get to hell and gone from there.

Do they *need* a genus and species?
Really? How about Scarfyou Maximus?
Hey, they'll eat you and drain yer
Monster size Big Gulp cup of swamp water too!

Tra Tra Tra Tra

Tra Tra Tra Tra, cryptid giant
lemur of Madagascar,
surviving Paleopropithecus
or Hadropithicus? Who knows?

You never come close enough
for any cryptozoologist to tell.
Just shake that big proboscis,
lean on yer knuckles and chuckle.

As if to say we homo sapiens
aren's so muckin' futch ourselves.
Chew animal parts and limp vegetables,
drink stuff that makes us slur and stumble.

Laugh, slap hands and backs,
leave the campfire as if we had
mismatched-length gams, poorer
eyesight than a star-nosed mole.

And they want Tra to reach
for a hand of bananas, tempt him
to get in the back of their van.
Prattle on about new digs in the city.

Sounds like Tra gets a tree and rope swing.
Like he doesn't already have a jungle!
A cement pond, when he's got rivers
and lakes! So they feed him! Big deal!

Anything he needs to eat he can find myself,
thank you very much! Bananas that taste
like real bananas, roots and berries. Don't need
tube steaks or beans. They make Tra toot!

No, you can keep your three squares
and heated cage. He's got the sky –
and stars. Look up and you'll see
much more than will fit in a box.

O.K. it's kinda neat that
the pictures change and flicker
quicker than he can turn the stars
on or off your indoor squawk box.

If he gets tired, he can just close his eyes
and go to sleep. Full technicolour dreams
don't do it for you, Holmes?
too bad, so sad...

Likely extinct?!
That's what scientists think?!
Well, here's a fresh
Kamchata patty steaming
Bergman's Bear's rebuttal

*

Snake or saurian?
The Badagui presents
a long neck either way.
A coiled snake that eats fruit?
Not unless he needs to toot.

*

The Liger is
Half tiger, half lion, mate.
Values his spots:
the better per ounce
in concealing his pounce.

*

*

you think I smell?!
you stink of money, Bud –
soiled bales of the stuff!
(first translated fragment of
Sasquatch Musings)

*

De Loy's Ape

De Loy's Ape
sat on a crate
mouth agape
propped by a stake
willy to the weather

Could be a gibbon
with tail hidden
or a new world ape!
Go on and gawk! Mock away!
De Loy's *in* a crate either way

*

Short-faced Booger Bears
get up in your face
with ape-like aplomb.
Shock you just long enough
to swat your head clean off!

*

Ratman of Southend
has a den under his bridge
Eats hapless homeless

*

McFarlane's Bear –
corpse in the Smithsonian
Half polar/ half grizzly
or a new species? Too bad
we didn't collect its feces.

Darrel Dogigator

No!? Dogigator was a fake?!
A statue, in fact. Dog shape clad
in alligator hide standing on all fours
behind the fern fronds hiding his dinner bowl.

Big alligator grin displaying a full grill
in shadow. (No cell phones or flashlights allowed.)
Stuffed reptilian McGuffin in the scaly
altogether. (Teeth sparkle in any weather.)

Arf! Arf! Arf! you wanna say,
or toss him an unwrapped Twinkie –
something that will last a thousand years
if he doesn't scoop or snap it up first.

Red Rain

In India and Sri Lanka
during the last rainy season
blood red rain fell night and day.

Scientists examined the water,
expecting to find dust particles,
but discovered live cells!

Reproducing live cells –
with no DNA/ RNA process.
Ergo, not from this planet, Janet!

It gets better. Radioactive!
Able to reproduce in extreme
climate conditions. Ice cap or not.

Thought to be particles of a meteor —
from an outside atmosphere explosion
– just before the arrival of the red rain.

But no. Maybe not hitch-hikers,
what with the incendiary heat
of a meteor burning up ...

unless they came flash frozen
in an alien blister pack
of some shell we know diddly about.

just excreted via
alien technology – through
a worm hole *a la carte.*

Get ready, Freddie!
This is gonna get heady!
Alien spawn floating along

seas, rivers, and streams ...
Not yer men's adventure
exploration magazine story.

Maybe gather the eggs up –
Free caviar for all the world's
People, bro. Mega-endorphin

biological injection, mate!
Maybe some alien data virus
is ridin' shotgun. Caviar for breakfast!

I mean, if they're gonna infect us anyway,
We'll need psychonaut pioneers
like we did in the sixties, man!

Could be big! Installing alien
biological chips... . The species
could use an upgrade for sure!

Qualupalik

Long lanky hair, green skin, long fingernails –
the better to snag badly- behaved little boys
and girls, the Inuit tell their kids. Qualupalik's
gonna snatch 'em off the snow and ice
and take them to their underwater lair!

Don't worry; they drown you first,
Then hull your skull for fresh brains.
Yum. Yum. Warm and wiggly, so
Scrumpdillyishish! Ears and lips,
Noses, and toes. Can't get enough of those!

Disobedient kids emit disagreeable smells –
Just the right mix of piss and vinegar
that Qualupaliks love and can easily sniff out
with their long protuberant noses.
No escape then! It's dinner time!

Fresh kid and fucus! Kelp and kiddly pie!
They'll pick their teeth with yer bones
when they're done! And belch a bubble
big and noxious enough to crack the ice –
Not once. Not twice. But thrice!

A sheet of ice won't stop 'em.
They'll smash through and grab you.
No time to pray please someone save me!
They'll have a wad of you churning
in their chubby cheeks by then!

The Kalanoros of Madagascar

The Kalanoros of Madagascar
are shy retiring hominids
that stand five and a half feet tall –

at most! Covered in course
brown-black hair with
quill-like spines down their backs,

they mostly traipse about
the largely uninhabited interior,
root for roots and eat berries.

Might paw a fish out of a stream,
but don't swat human brains
out of our heads – puh-lease!

They're peaceniks, primitive
hunter/gatherer relatives.
Don't eat humans as a rule.

Give them a wide berth to be sure.
Maybe leave a hand of bananas
or a tray of mixed vegetables.

Don't get up in their faces
or insist on hunting them down
to bestow a genus and species name.

They ain't interested in selfies
or interviews either – assuming
you can find a common language.

No. Let 'em be. Running wild and free,
swingin' from vines, travellin' by
shank's mare over hill and dale.

Think of all the things they've avoided:
Bad government. Taxes. Gainful employment.
Bad haircuts. Fashion trends. Expensive digs.

Heck, join 'em! Get a pair or two
of furry jammies and hiking boots.
Leave the blunderbuss and tent at home.

Go on! Howl at the moon. Teach 'em about tools –
gut wrenches, plates, bowls.
Get yer own face down in a bowl and grunt.

Amali

Don't dilly dally, Mr. Amali.
Show yourself, please! We need
a cryptid critter such as your highness
to get classified, given a genus and species
so the cryptozoologists can say,
"See, we told you so. Dinosaurs exist!"
I insist. One grunt for *yes*. C'mon!
Flash a little grill and rubbery hide.
Smile for the cell phone, like you give a damn.
Your cuz, Mokele M'bembe, in the Congo
has already been the subject of a Hollywood movie.
With your looks, you won't be flippin' burgers,
trust me. You'll have your own crib and waterslide!
All the babes you want tossin' you croissants
from poolside. Scamper in the back of my pick-up.
I've got all the Scooby snacks you could ever need
for the trip to yer new bachelor pad, Dad.

Gwyllgi

Giant mastiff with blazing red eyes,
AKA Dog of Darkness for those
who can't handle all the consonants
in Llandegla, Wales. Demon Dog?

Yeah, well, this one goes double
on the trouble, dudes; you doan wanna
run into him on a dark path.
You can't run fast enough.

Yer basically an aperitif – unless
there are two or three of you;
then yer tapas, assorted treats
from yer mother's own bakery!

Gwyllgi likes to gut his victims,
stand among the glut of intestines
to dine. Hulls yer skull last.
Brains are such as nice repast.

Jorogumo

Jorogumo's no Anansi imp;
ain't no Japanese tarantula.
Can shape shift into a femme fatale –

an any-kind-you-fancy Nancy
or Betty Noir. Buxom brunette
with or without mole? Lusty surfer blonde?

Or black, high cheek and long-boned –
the kind you wanna take home to ma.
Exotic Asian – whatever amazin' cliché

you got goin', she'll materialize for you.
Imagine the crookin' capabilities
of eight fingers in two. That hullabaloo.

She's gonna bleed you of your every resource
and then suck your soul thorough a hole
you didn't know you had. Lust and pride? Poof!

She'll ride you out to the sunset
and suck every bit of succulence
outta yer tired hide. Then abide

as a plump spider in a twelve-foot nest
in the forest between trees. Don't do
to get on yer knees when you sproing into that net!

Homo Sapiens III

Come on you alien geneticists!
Get crackin'! Homo S II is a bust!
You absolutely must start splicing
our chromosomes with alien DNA!

We've been waitin' ages for an upgrade!
If you could work on the flight or fight
module; maybe shave a few molecules
off the violent action/reaction circuit...

That'd be great! Maybe re-ignite
the round-the-campfire-camaraderie
pilot light? Give our couch spud
genes the heave-ho. Hey! Jack in!

A little more ROM and RAM,
if you please, Mr. Melon Head –
Hey, you can have some of my hair.
It's falling out anyway and you grays –

Well, let's just say you might wanna
doff the lamé space tights and
get mammalary once in a while
in proper simian style. Your arms are twigs!

There, I said it. Neck too. How the heck
does it support that big melon of yours?!
Just sayin'... You might wanna clone a
few sapiens genes, splice 'em into your own.

Hey! You got any common sense
in any of those cranial cookie jars
you keep in the fridge? Most homo s
citizens could use a pinch in the mix.

Just sayin ... Super size my pia mater, dude;
I'll give you a little attitude –
maybe a set of weights to start you off.
Yer gonna need a sense of humor down here too.

By all means, help yourselves to the cow parts.
The blood – plasma, the works, Any giblets
you wanna avail yourselves of. Brains?
Well, maybe not the brains. They're primitive.

Old technology to you boys, eh? Say,
you don't suppose I could get an upgrade
on this old chassis? Maybe better fittings
and valves? I'm starting to creak like the tin man.

The golden years suck! Homo S II sucks!
We've raped the planet, man! Maybe we
should blow ourselves up and give the cockroach
a chance. Maybe a layin' on of alien hands ... .

Paranormal Parasites

Paranormal parasites
got the plasma in plastic
take-out bags!

Old hags
and homeless hosts
give up the most:

Sell their own blood
to vampiric ghosts
and plum disappear!

Sorry, Cyrus,
you've got the virus!
Have a hit of this ...

Temporary bliss
Better 'n' breakfast bagels.
Hey, Mabel, Black Label!

Paranormal parasites
Suck the O and R
Right out of orgone.

We're gone, baby!
To the spare parts
sports emporium.

Saucy saucer hostess
gonna pass our dirty genes
to some underdressed launderess.

Paranormal parasites
sure got the bite on us.
Ain't no ray gun or blunderbuss

we can turn on them.
Nope. We're done, Clem:
intergalactic toast.

So enjoy the half-life
at half mast.
Nothin's made to last.

Stand agog and gape
at the insectoids
behind the drapes.

This ain't Oz
or the North Pole,
and dey ain't Santa's elves!

Paranormal parasites!
Gonna suck the life
Right out of us, Gus.

Don't need a haberdasher
or tailor for this
vampiric caper.

Don't need blood per se,
just a little Chinese Chi,
a little plasma, if you please.

Paranormal parasites
prefer take-out to
a sit-down dinner anytime.

Will scarf you on the fly!
Gas, solid, liquid –
it don't matter.

You can forgo the platter.
Don't need mammal matter,
just a big energy drink

of reconstituted molecules
through any pore or orifice.
Ogone on ice, so nice!

Big Gulp?!

Human flesh?!
Yer what got us into this mess!
Why would I wanna
mack on any part of you?
Bad gas. But I digress…

Need I say
he didn't *say* that exactly
but I got it!
Caddy wants you to know
yer too flabby, might have mites!

Tunnepfiefer

Tunnepfiefer –
Tunnel Piper to you,
my English-speaking friend.

Hideous mole from the U-balm.
Not a good pet unless you want
one crawling through your sewer pipes.

Too big to flush down the loo
when yer done being fascinated
with its star nose, no see-em gaze.

It's his whistle, not his bite
that'll have you pullin' cotton
out of your car seat cushions!

His whistle'll shake the coating
offa galvanized roof nails.
You'll need ear plugs for this gig.

Findin' one at any hour you
wanna be awake may be a problem.
What's good five-foot mole bait?

Why do you wanna capture one?
Picture no good? Witnesses' sketches
got no extractable bone marrow DNA?

Gotcha. O.K., let's start
with a big net, cop-size flash lights,
extra batteries, and a bazooka.

Megalania Mania

Megalania mania in Queensland!
Large goannas spotted in the forests
of Kuranda! Giant lizards, mate!
Twice the size of yer Komodo dragon.
A million smacketroos if you can bag one.

You'll need a bigger gun than that
gat you're packin'. This ain't
the big city; we're talkin' BIG LIZARD!
Runs faster than a man can uphill
and his sense of smell is most astute.

Think land shark. Those kinda rip-you-
in-half incisors. They as much as sniff
yer rotten meat, they're on ya like
stink on shit. Yer an indeterminate blur
of assorted body parts, mate. Brain paté.

No, you need a waist cannon, my man!
Something that will blow a hole you can
see next week through at two
hundred feet. You gotta be sharp, silent
as a slowly released fart on a leather car seat.

E's got a poxy drool too, he does:
one bite and yer immobilized by
a noxious bacterium or fungus growin'
on his sizable incisors. Get that inside
yer bloodstream and yer basically toast.

You gotta wanna get this beast
before it gets wind of you is what
I'm layin' down here. Yer with me, right?
Better blunderbuss, Gus. No gorbie togs.
No neon or after shave. Get what I'm sayin'?

We're not talkin' some dumbass
T-Rex that wants to eat you gently
like a cob of corn between delicate mitts.
Smaller, yes, but intelligent – a whole
other level of horror – on four fleet feet!

All they found of the last intrepid warrior
was his cell phone. Indigestible aperitif,
apparently. Efficient if not tidy eaters!
A million razbutniks, buddy, whaddaya say?
(No you don't want to see the cell phone snaps.)

The Slaugh

Be wary of the Slaugh, my friend.
They'll fill a kid's jungle gym
or school swing set the way

they did in Hitchcock's **The Birds**!
A flock of blackbirds can descend
like darkness itself. Envelope you.

If you're lucky, they'll drop you
in some cushy hay bail or bay,
let you come to, brain and limbs intact.

Wiser about how you regard Mother Nature
and her minions, for sure; your own teeth
chattering as you regale us with the tale.

I wouldn't chance a return visit though.
Have a P.E.I. potato or two, a cuppa joe
and think about it a bit anyway.

Gbahali (Bar Lye)

The Kahai River,
Liberia is my hang.
Half croc/half monitor,
don't drag my belly
when I run after you.

Love homo s. meat!
Forearms fit like corn cobs
between my short front feet.
I could gnaw on you pirogue-
floating *hors d'ouvres* all week.

Kajanok

Kajanok, giant
underwater spider
the size of a Huntsman
hunts silver fish fry.

Weaves invisible
underwater webs
of fine-spun silk
fry bungle into

while combing the reef
for a little food themselves,
poor babies! No maybes:
they're invited to dinner tonight!

No reservation
required of guests
who find themselves
the slurp du jour.

First, spidey dresses
you in the finest silk suit
and tie (required
by the management.)

Then he bites you –
just a playful nibble.
Injects a little juice
to make you loose and limber.

You relax. Think you're
too corpulent anyway.
You'll thank Spidey for taking
you down a hat and waist size –

two, three waist sizes
if you sit still and wait.
That's it. Flap those gills
a little more slowly.

Grouper grope. Big one.
That's it. You drift off.
No need to flap yer gums ...
just slowly surely succumb.

How was that then?
I'm sophonsified. You?
Well, just look at you!
A shadow of yourself!

Leftovers are better –
hang around for lunch?
I can't believe how good
you look in that suit!

no intelligent life
on this planet to report
Bigfoot boards his craft

*

All the brochures brag
"selfies with serpent here!"
Champ got no memo

*

The greys hard at work
at crispr cloning cryptids
shoulda stopped at reptiles

*

sphinx on Mars! You mean
the visitors wanted us
to think one was ours?

*

Mugwump's stumped –
Lake Tamiskaming for lunch
or hang up his humps?

*

Rougarou,
über booger werewolf doofus
wants fast food now!
Toss him a pizza, burger,
anything but human flesh

*

Spiffy Ziphius –
tupper-tight grin, owl eyes,
slipped roll call a while.
Couvier's Beaked Whale, last ziph
to give us the slip, grins still

*

you're safe: Mugwump's not
fond of homo s kebabs
nor blue burritos
fibreglass ain't fibre
and canoes too hard to pass

*

Batatut!
You stink!
Gotta learn to scoop…

*

Nabau's on the nod
best let him sleep in
at one-hundred feet

*

King Cobra
yer a BIG snake! Can I
interest you in steak?

Hibagon

Harry Hibagon hails from Mt. Hilba
in Hiroshima Prefecture, Japan.
He's a no-nonsense, short, hairy guy
who minds his business wrapping lamb.

The face mask hides his ugly mug
as he works behind the deli case
and takes orders for humus,
cottage cheese, and miso paste.

They say after his skin melted
in Hiroshima, his skin grew back
black and hairy. Hence his adopted name.
No! No! wanted to ink a contract,

but with a face that looked like a pug's
that had been chasing parked cars,
he might as well have been a werewolf
or the Monster Minister from Mars.

Had a few surgeon roles in his time –
bit parts, really, when a director needed
a hairy arm, dark, trusting eyes,
the mask-on rule always heeded.

No wonder he gave up acting
and took up hacking limbs, slicing meat.
If he mumbles enough praise, the customers
will keep him off the street.

He might only make a living wage,
but with toxic levels of auto fumes
so high in Hiroshima, no one notices
the mask. He slides in and outta rooms.

Poor guy. Where do you troll the Internet
to find a date with a bearded babe?
He needs Social Media like he needs
another deep black hole in his face.

Harry Hibagon was woebegone –
beyond **No No**'s taunt of hirsute-less bliss,
beyond the reach of fellow circus freaks
who mugged for spit and a hateful hiss.

What could he do, besides slice meat
for a livin'? It's not like folks were kind
or particularly givin'. Given his druthers,
he'd slice 'em up as mystery meat and hind.

He's not a monster. Just looks like one.
Maybe you oughta sit in the sun
until yer carcass looks like stewin' meat.
Tell him then, how yer so hot, yer the one.

You wanna Sasquatch? O.K., he'll drop his arms
and shuffle some. Throw him cabbages,
he'll bowl for dollars along with you.
Forget yer wisdom-packed adages… .

He's Harry Hibagon – Fur Face to you.
Slap him in a cage. Let 'im carve flutes
or sell candles on yer streets. He's no freak!
He's Harry Hibagon. Dig his nail-pullin' glutes!

Reptoid Encounter

O.K., dude, whatchew gonna do
if some reptoid in the road holds
his own and refuses to book it
into the tulies? Runs right at *your* car?

He's clawin' and clamberin' the hood.
You'd be thinkin', *If I grab my rifle*
and shoot him through the windshield
and I don't *kill him, he's got me.*

You'd tramp on the accelerator and pull
some crazy ass turns before you shook
him off. You'd leave him on a roadside rail.
The front-end damage would be extensive.

Better than you, for sure. You couldn't
imagine what this lizard man would have
done to your thin hide, never mind the gash,
big red splash and plash of intestines.

What did he *look* like?! Like death
comin' at me with the speed and
power of a freight train. Hominid features
scrunched up in a slavering sneer.

Face-for-radio reptoid Elvis.
I dunno. Scarey and fixated
on my gizzards. Dog-toothed,
scaly, intent to get in and get me.

Jesus, I dunno! Its legs came
out of its sides like a lizard's,
not down from a pelvis, like a human's.
Wasn't wearin' winkle pickers.

I didn't *want* to see him droolin'
in front of the steering wheel a quarter
inch of glass away. His eyes though –
they were full of luminous intelligence.

Better him hanging over a guard rail.
You'd be outta there faster than
shit through a goose. Gone before the sun
could set on another day. To the nearest saloon.

Gooned, all bedraggled and befuddled,
if not drooling, wide-eyed, slack-jawed
like some Pavlovian dog yourself. Every
pissed and shit-squish pattied inch of you.

An Argentine Alien

An Argentine alien
has rustled the bushes
and stepped into view.

He's not like me or you.
He's but four foot two –
Kinda green, maybe blue.

I'm so outta here,
whatever this thing is
that ain't exactly clear.

Got a low rez fuzzy gif
of some kinda elvish imp,
but I didn't stop to swap IDs.

Coulda got here in a saucer…
He smelled bad; I nearly tossed 'er,
But, as I say, I beat a retreat.

Loose as a goose,
arms furiously pumping
their own stiff green gallop!

You wanna go back
And check the ground
For tripod marks and radiation?!

Why not just ask Santa
if he's short an elf?
(Note to self: Am-scray

this pop stand Bay – beh!
Doan wanna be off the radar.
I *like* a short leash!)

Veggie Man

Veggie Man's
deceptive thin-armed snag
of your wrist stoppeth
the two of you cold
as refrigerated veggies.

Let him vanish
in a mist on a mountain.
Be stunned and amazed
and shut up for the rest
of yer disbelieving days.

The Monster of Lake Totu

Diablo ballena –
Devil Whale of Lake Totu
the locals call it.

Black head of an ox,
big as a whale.
A living dinosaur?

Mosasaur maybe
or living Livyatan?
Thought extinct, but not?

Sunbathers don't buy
the story and tan to their
heart's content in the sand.

Have walked the strand sans
incident this century.
Does that mean it's dead?

Too bad if it is!
Nothing's better than
a good scare from a big boat!

Yamakachi

Yamagutchi!
Yamagotchee!
Yamakachi!

Musta-stuffed-you
in-a-drawer-
and-forgot-chu.

Couldn't turn you off
or hack the pace of feeding
your every need.

In any case,
glad you escaped.
Please don't eat me.

Derrider Roadkill

Derrider roadkill's
gotta be simian remains –
ape-like face – no dog!
First evidence of Napes –
North American Apes!

Quick! Get him in
a deepfreeze or bottle
of formaldehyde!
Tan or preserve his hide;
Don't incinerate his ass!

Please! Think DNA!
No escapee from a zoo
or circus. I checked.
He's a specimen at least
of interest to science!

A hairy hominid!
One of us, Gus.
Get it in yer skull!
Not to be cremated
or buried just yet ...

Roadkill ain't
landfill, dude! He's
someone's, some thing's son.
Look! Those ain't Betty Davis
eyes, maybe, but, hey ...

Multiverses, eh?

(for Rob Redgrave)

Multiverses, eh?
Time warps and wormholes
between 'em. Asteroids to avoid ...

Sounds like a video game
or pinball for the souls
of the elderly, maybe –

No coin slots but our eyes,
ears, and mouths, This amazed
gray's ready to iron away

the wrinkles in time. Socks and slippers
standard uniform on the wards.
Windows still barred; glass, cold.

Like the concept. Got a ride?
This universe, this globe, this place
is getting' stale. Which button do I push?

Can I choose
time and place of entry?
Departure a button away?

Is shank's mare available
above the clouds and gone
from here? In any hemisphere?

I liked this universe fine
when I was nine. Can I go there?
In my jammies with my Granny?

Watching something on KOMO
Channel 4 (Seattle was it?)
Something my parents couldn't get.

Only available by antennae!
Forget twiddling rabbit ears!
When donuts were sixty cents a dozen?

Can I walk up the hill
to the Rockhound Shop
and buy a piece of malachite?

Can I have it fashioned
into an amulet to ward off goofs?
Change gender for the halibut?

Might be fun! Heck,
I'm old; no point in growing mould!
Gender re-assignment isn't included?

How about a vehicle change?
A younger one or someone new?
A sassy lassie, new chassis?

I'd jump the tube
for a new lube any day!
Where's the chute? Do I look cute?

If I twiddle my gray curls?
Simonize my bald dome?
What's it cost in soul transfer tokens?

I gotta shit load
from the sale of the house!
I'm ready, Freddie! Press **Outta Here**!

humankind –
earth's biggest
viral load

THE ARTIST

Carla Stein's illustrations appear in chapbooks, on walls and on-line including *The Belladonna, Stonecoast Review, Lemonspouting, The Starlight Scifaiku Review* and *The Lotus Tree Literary Review*. She's in the garden when not making art or writing her own poetry. Find more of her work at: www.roaeriestudio.com

Manufactured by Amazon.ca
Acheson, AB